Miranda v. Arizona (1966)

By SUSAN DUDLEY GOLD

TWENTY-FIRST CENTURY
BOOKS
A Division of
Henry Holt and Company

New York

To John, with love.

Twenty-First Century Books
A Division of Henry Holt and Company, Inc.
115 West 18th Street
New York, NY 10011

Henry Holt® and colophon are trademarks of
Henry Holt and Company, Inc.
Publishers since 1866

Library of Congress Cataloging-in-Publication Data
Gold, Susan Dudley.
Miranda v. Arizona (1966) : suspects' rights / Susan Dudley Gold. — 1st ed.
p. cm. — (Supreme Court decisions)
Includes bibliographical references and index.
Summary: On June 13, 1966, a divided Supreme Court ruled that suspects must be informed of their rights, including the right to remain silent and the right to counsel, before they are questioned by the police.
1. Miranda, Ernesto—Trials, litigation, etc.—Juvenile literature. 2. Right to counsel—United States—Juvenile literature. 3. Confession (Law)—United States—Juvenile literature. 4. Police questioning—United States—Juvenile literature. [1. Miranda, Ernesto—Trials, litigation, etc. 2. Right to counsel. 3. Police questioning. 4. Civil rights—History.]
I. Title. II.Title: Miranda versus Arizona. (1966) III. Series: Supreme Court decisions (New York, N.Y.)
KF228.M57G65 1995   345.73'056— dc20   94-45045
[347.30556]   CIP AC

Photo Credits
Photo on page 42 © Earl McCartney, *Arizona Republic*, The Phoenix Newspapers.
All other photos provided by AP / Wide World Photos.

Design
Tina Tarr-Emmons

Typesetting and Layout
Custom Communications

ISBN 0-8050-3915-5
First Edition 1995

Printed in the United States of America
All first editions are printed on acid-free paper ∞.
10 9 8 7 6 5 4 3 2 1

Contents

Mary T. Quinn displays an original copy of the Bill of Rights that she found in a filing cabinet in the Rhode Island State House Archives.

The Bill of Rights

Amendment I

Congress shall make no law respecting an establishment of religion, or prohibiting the free exercise thereof; or abridging the freedom of speech, or of the press; or the right of the people peaceably to assemble, and to petition the Government for a redress of grievances.

Amendment II

A well regulated Militia, being necessary to the security of a free State, the right of the people to keep and bear Arms, shall not be infringed.

Amendment III

No Soldier shall, in time of peace be quartered in any house, without the consent of the Owner, nor in time of war, but in a manner to be prescribed by law.

Amendment IV

The right of the people to be secure in their persons, houses, papers, and effects, against unreasonable searches and seizures, shall not be violated, and no Warrants shall issue, but upon probable cause, supported by Oath or affirmation, and particularly describing the place to be searched, and the persons or things to be seized.

Amendment V

No person shall be held to answer for a capital, or otherwise infamous crime, unless on a presentment or indictment of a Grand Jury, except in cases arising in the land or naval forces, or in the Militia, when in actual service in time of War or public danger; nor shall any person be subject for the same offence to be twice put in jeopardy of life or limb, nor shall be compelled in any criminal case to be a witness against himself, nor be deprived of life, liberty, or property, without due process of law; nor shall private property be taken for public use without just compensation.

Amendment VI

In all criminal prosecutions, the accused shall enjoy the right to a speedy and public trial, by an impartial jury of the State and district wherein the crime shall have been committed; which district shall have been previously ascertained by law, and to be informed of the nature and cause of the accusation; to be confronted with the witnesses against him; to have compulsory process for obtaining witnesses in his favor, and to have the assistance of counsel for his defence.

Amendment VII

In Suits at common law, where the value in controversy shall exceed twenty dollars, the right of trial by jury shall be preserved, and no fact tried by a jury shall be otherwise re-examined in any Court of the United States, than according to the rules of the common law.

Amendment VIII

Excessive bail shall not be required, nor excessive fines imposed, nor cruel and unusual punishments inflicted.

Amendment IX

The enumeration in the Constitution of certain rights shall not be construed to deny or disparage others retained by the people.

Amendment X

The powers not delegated to the United States by the Constitution, nor prohibited by it to the States, are reserved to the States respectively, or to the people.

Amendment XIV (ratified July 28, 1868)

Section 1. All persons born or naturalized in the United States and subject to the jurisdiction thereof, are citizens of the United States and of the State wherein they reside. No State shall make or enforce any law which shall abridge the privileges or immunities of citizens of the United States; nor shall any State deprive any person of life, liberty, or property, without due process of law; nor deny to any person within its jurisdiction the equal protection of the laws.

Section 2. Representatives shall be apportioned among the several States according to their respective numbers, counting the whole number of persons in each State, excluding Indians not taxed. But when the right to vote at any election for the choice of electors for President and Vice President of the United States, Representatives in Congress, the Executive and Judicial officers of a State, or the members of the Legislature thereof, is denied to any of the male inhabitants of such State, being twenty-one years of age, and citizens of the United States, or in any way abridged, except for participation in rebellion, or other crime, the basis of representation therein shall be reduced in the proportion which the number of such male citizens shall bear to the whole number of male citizens twenty-one years of age in such State.

Section 3. No person shall be a Senator or Representative in Congress, or elector of President and Vice President, or hold any office, civil or military, under the United States, or under any State, who, having previously taken an oath, as a member of Congress, or as an officer of the United States, or as a member of any State legislature, or as an executive or judicial officer of any State, to support the Constitution of the United States, shall have engaged in insurrection or rebellion against the same, or given aid or comfort to the enemies thereof. But Congress may by a vote of two-thirds of each House, remove such disability.

Section 4. The validity of the public debt of the United States, authorized by law, including debts incurred for payment of pensions and bounties for services in suppressing insurrection or rebellion, shall not be questioned. But neither the United States nor any State shall assume or pay any debt or obligation incurred in aid of insurrection or rebellion against the United States, or any claim for the loss or emancipation of any slave; but all such debts, obligations and claims shall be held illegal and void.

Section 5. The Congress shall have power to enforce, by appropriate legislation, the provisions of this article.

A Most Significant Decision

The criminal goes free, if he must, but it is the law that sets him free. Nothing can destroy a government more quickly than its failure to observe its own laws, or worse, its disregard of the charter of its own existence.[1]

—**Justice Tom C. Clark**
Mapp v. Ohio

On June 13, 1966, Chief Justice Earl Warren read a 61-page opinion that would rewrite police manuals throughout the nation. In the 5 to 4 decision, the Supreme Court ruled that suspects must be informed of their rights, including the right to remain silent and the right to counsel, before police questioned them. If suspects confessed before being warned of their rights, according to the ruling, the confessions could not be used at trial.

The decision overturned the convictions of three men accused of crimes ranging from robbery to rape and murder and upheld the reversal of another man's conviction for bank robbery. The four cases, grouped under *Miranda v. Arizona*, led to establishment of the *Miranda* warnings, required by the Court to inform suspects questioned in criminal cases of their rights.

In issuing its decisions, the Court usually leaves the states and lower court judges to devise ways to meet the requirements of the rulings. In *Miranda v. Arizona*, however, Warren gave detailed instructions to police on what they were to say to suspects. The *Miranda* warning used by police today follows the wording in the decision almost exactly:

> You have the right to remain silent. Anything you say can and will be used against you in a court of law. You have the right to talk to a lawyer and have him present while you're being questioned. If you cannot afford to hire a lawyer, one will be appointed to represent you before any questioning, if you wish one.[2]

The ruling ignited a fierce controversy between those who saw the decision as a safeguard against overzealous police interrogation and those who feared the *Miranda* warnings would hamper police efforts to fight crime. The famous defense lawyer Melvin Belli said the *Miranda* ruling "may be the most significant decision in the field of criminal law ever written by an appellate judicial body."[3]

The battle over *Miranda* played a major role in the 1968 presidential election of Richard M. Nixon and led to a showdown between Congress and the Supreme Court. Despite the efforts of a president and Congress to overturn the decision, *Miranda* warnings remain today as a safeguard against police intimidation.

This is the story of the events that led the Court to reach the historic decision and of the young suspect whose name is forever linked to the cause of suspects' rights.

CHAPTER ONE

The Confession of an Innocent Man

> *If the government becomes a law-breaker, it breeds contempt for law; it invites every man to become a law unto himself; it invites anarchy.*[1]
>
> —Justice Louis D. Brandeis
> *Olmstead v. United States*

On August 28, 1963, the bodies of two young women were found in their Upper East Side apartment in New York City. They had been stabbed so savagely that the blades of two of the three kitchen knives used in the attack had been broken. Their bodies had been tied together, ankles to wrists. Three smashed soda bottles lay on the floor. The apartment had been ransacked, but nothing appeared to be missing.

The case caused a furor in the city and the rest of the country. One of the victims, twenty-one-year-old Janice Wylie, was the daughter of a prominent advertising executive and television writer. He had found his daughter's body and called police to the scene. Her uncle was the novelist

George Whitmore Jr., nineteen, is pictured at a Brooklyn police station after admitting he killed Janice Wylie and Emily Hoffert.

Philip Wylie. Janice Wylie had worked as a copy girl at *Newsweek* magazine and aspired to be an actress. *Newsweek* offered $10,000 for information leading to the arrest of her killer.

The second victim, Wylie's twenty-three-year-old roommate, Emily Hoffert, had been hired as an elementary-school teacher in a Long Island school. The daughter of a Minneapolis surgeon, she was a Smith College graduate described by the *New York Times* as a "serious woman."[2]

Press coverage of the murders was intense. Detailed reports of the killings and the murder scene were followed by stories on the police department's inability to find the killer. The case was characterized as "one of the city's most baffling crimes of recent years."[3] For months the police could find no clues. They questioned more than 1,000 people about the slayings.

Then, on April 25, 1964, a young black man named George Whitmore Jr. confessed to the crime. Described by reporters as a "slender, near-sighted 19-year-old drifter,"[4] Whitmore had been arrested early the morning of April 24 for an unrelated robbery and attempted rape of a nurse named Elba Borrero. As part of their routine questioning, police officers asked Whitmore about other crimes that had taken place near the site of the attempted rape. Police said Whitmore "confessed readily" to the slashing death of another woman, Minnie Edmonds, who had been killed April 14.[5]

Police Detective Edward Bulger was at the police station during Whitmore's questioning. Bulger, who had been assigned to cover the Wylie case, noticed a photograph of a girl that Whitmore had been carrying in his pocket. The detective thought the girl looked like Wylie.

Bulger asked Whitmore about the photograph. He said he had found the photograph in a garbage dump near his family's home in Wildwood, New Jersey. Bulger, who thought Whitmore had taken the photograph from Wylie's apartment, continued the questioning. Officers came and went throughout the day and the following night. Sometimes they asked questions, sometimes they made statements. Early the next morning, Whitmore signed a 60-page statement confessing to murdering three people: Edmonds, Wylie, and Hoffert. He had been at the police station for 26 hours.

At Whitmore's arraignment later that day, he recanted all three confessions. During arraignment, a suspect is taken before a judge and told of the charges against him or her. At the arraignment, the suspect can plead innocent or guilty or make no plea. Whitmore's court-appointed lawyer, Jerome Leftow, met with Whitmore for the first time in the courtroom and told the judge that his client had been forced to confess.

The confession made front-page news in the next day's *New York Times*. Under the headline, YOUTH IS ACCUSED IN WYLIE SLAYING, a photograph showed a dazed Whitmore, being led from a Brooklyn police station to be arraigned.[6]

Police said Whitmore had divulged details of the Wylie-Hoffert slayings that had not been made public. One source said the youth had described how he broke the blades of two of the knives used in the killing by crushing them with his heel. Police said that Whitmore had denied ever reading any of the numerous stories about the killings.

Wylie's father expressed relief that the killer had been caught. But Philip Wylie was quoted as saying, "It sounds to me like a guy who got scared into a confession or wanted to make a name for himself."[7] He also questioned whether the slight young man—Whitmore was 5'5" tall and weighed 140 pounds—would have the strength to break the knives with his heel when police officers testing similar knives had been unable to break them.

The judge ordered Whitmore held without bail for a hearing scheduled April 30. He had no previous criminal record. A police officer in Wildwood who knew Whitmore said he was surprised by the charges.

Trial was set for November in the robbery and attempted rape case. Whitmore was formally charged, or indicted, by a grand jury in the Wylie-Hoffert murders May 6, 1964. He was expected to face trial in that case sometime in 1965. He would be tried for the Edmonds murder in April 1965.

From May until October, Whitmore was held at the Bellevue Psychiatric Hospital, where he was tested and questioned. During that time, he continued to say he had not committed the crimes. Tests of Whitmore as a seventh-grade student in Wildwood recorded him as having an IQ of 60. Later tests at Bellevue recorded his IQ as 90. Both scores are below the normal level. Whitmore had left school before finishing the eighth grade.

At Bellevue, Whitmore wrote that he had confessed because he was afraid ("squared") of the police officers questioning him. "I was so squared that I was shakeing all over. And before I know it, I was saying yes. I was so squared if they would have told me [my] name was tom, dick or harry I would have said yes."[8]

In November, Whitmore went on trial for the robbery and attempted rape of Elba Borrero. Taking the stand, the young man testified that police officers had punched him 50 times in the stomach during questioning after he was arrested. "I broke down and shook my head to everything they said," Whitmore told the court.[9] Police officers denied the charge, and New York Supreme Court Acting Justice David Malbin ruled that Whitmore had given the confessions voluntarily.

On November 19, 1964, a jury of 12 men found Whitmore guilty of both charges. The victim had identified him as her attacker in court. But

Whitmore's lawyer noted that it had been dark and stormy the night of the crime, that Borrero had lost her glasses in the struggle, and that the original alarm issued over the police radio had described the suspect as heavier and taller than Whitmore. The lawyer also pointed out that the victim had never mentioned the pockmarks that dotted Whitmore's face. Jurors at the trial admitted they had known that Whitmore was also accused in the Wylie-Hoffert murders.

Whitmore was taken to the Brooklyn House of Detention for Men to await sentencing. He faced a ten-year jail sentence for the attempted rape and a five-year sentence for the assault.

Preparing for the Wylie-Hoffert and Edmonds trials, Whitmore's lawyer continued to contend that Whitmore had given his confession to all three crimes under duress.

Two weeks after Whitmore had been indicted in the Wylie-Hoffert case, detectives discovered that the photograph the young man had carried with him was not of Wylie. Throughout the summer, they had tried to track down the girl in the photo. Finally, in December, they traced the scene to a picnic area near Wildwood. The detectives identified the girl, who had been at a school picnic. The girl's friend acknowledged that she had thrown the photograph into the dump mentioned by Whitmore.

The detectives had also talked with a fifteen-year-old girl and her mother who knew Whitmore and said they had seen him the day of the murder in a hotel restaurant in Wildwood.

By this time, the detectives were beginning to think Whitmore was innocent.

In the meantime, another event was unfolding that would increase doubts about Whitmore's guilt. In October, a drug addict named Nathan Delaney had told police that another addict, Richard Robles, had killed

Richard Robles, twenty-two, stands in a New York City police station January 26, 1965, after he was taken into custody on a murder charge in the deaths of Janice Wylie and Emily Hoffert.

Wylie and Hoffert. After obtaining a court order, the police put wiretaps at the house Robles shared with his mother, at the house of Robles's girlfriend, and at Delaney's house. The resulting 200 hours of tapes provided powerful evidence of Robles's guilt. He was booked at police headquarters January 26, 1965, and charged with the crimes. An admitted heroin addict, Robles, twenty-two, was on parole after serving time for felonious assault.

On January 28, 1965, the district attorney's office dropped charges against Whitmore in the Wylie-Hoffert case. A member of the DA's staff told a *New York Times* reporter he blamed the mistaken indictment on the police department. "I am positive that the police prepared the confession for Whitmore," he said. "I am sure that the police were the ones who gave Whitmore all the details of the killings that he recited to our office."[10]

Another DA staff member agreed. "Call it what you want—brainwashing, hypnosis, fright. They made him give an untrue confession."[11] He added that the only thing he believed was true about police statements in the case was that they had not beaten the confession out of Whitmore. Police Commissioner Michael J. Murphy ordered a full investigation into events surrounding the Whitmore confession.

Meanwhile, Whitmore remained behind bars at the house of detention, awaiting a February 25 hearing on his motion for a new trial in the attempted rape case. He was still under indictment for the Edmonds slaying. But the revelation that he had been forced to confess in the Wylie-Hoffert case raised strong doubts about the validity of the confessions in the other cases.

Whitmore's trial for the Edmonds murder ended in a hung jury, and the charges were dismissed. He was freed on bail, awaiting a decision in the Borrero case. An appeals court overturned the jury's verdict in that case. But the tainted confession was used again in a second trial on the attempted rape. Again, the conviction was overturned by the appeals court. In the third trial, Whitmore's confession was not used. The jury, convinced by Borrero's testimony, once again voted to convict Whitmore.

This time, the appeals court upheld the verdict. The U.S. Supreme

20 George Whitmore Jr. hugs his mother, Birdene, after his release on bail July 13, 1966, while he appeals a five- to ten-year prison sentence in a conviction for attempted rape.

Court declined to hear Whitmore's appeal. He was taken to Green Haven Prison in New York to serve a five- to ten-year sentence.

A TV reporter, unconvinced of Whitmore's guilt, tracked down Borrero's sister-in-law in Puerto Rico. She swore that Borrero had described her attacker to her shortly after the attempted rape. Her description did not match that of Whitmore. Borrero had also picked out a mug shot at the police station of the man she said attacked her, but at that time there was no mug shot of Whitmore. He had never been in trouble with the law. Borrero changed her description of the attacker after she saw Whitmore, who had by then been picked up by the police.

The new evidence convinced the district attorney to seek Whitmore's release from jail. On April 10, 1973, Whitmore, now twenty-eight, was freed and the charges against him dropped. Both the district attorney and the judge who freed him called his treatment by the law enforcement system "a disgrace."[12] For nearly ten years, Whitmore had been held in psychiatric hospitals, spent four years in jail, and gone through four trials. He had been charged with three murders, attempted rape, and robbery. During his first trial, his father had suffered a heart attack in court. His mother had been hospitalized for stress during the ordeal.

George Whitmore Jr.'s case became a rallying point for those wary of heavy-handed police tactics, especially police treatment of minority suspects. Four days after police arrested Richard Robles in the Wylie-Hoffert case, a *New York Times* editorial called for an independent investigation of police behavior in the Whitmore case and abolishment of the death penalty. The editorial writer also cited the need for a comprehensive code of behavior for police departments in their dealings with suspects.[13]

A staff member in the DA's office noted that Whitmore might have been executed for a crime he hadn't committed if heavy publicity hadn't focused attention on the case. He blamed the police in Whitmore's case, but noted the DA's office might also be at fault in pressing for confessions. Normally, he said, police call the assistant DA after a suspect had made a statement. But sometimes a police detective calls the DA's office and says, "He hasn't broken yet, and it's been two hours," the staff member reported. He noted that the assistant DA might reply, "Call me again in an hour. Keep working."[14]

Other cases of forced confessions came to the attention of the public. At the same time Whitmore was enduring his ordeal, nineteen-year-old Alvin Mitchell was on trial for the murder of Barbara Karlik, who had been slain July 20, 1963, in New York City. Like Whitmore, Mitchell had confessed to police, then recanted. His trial in June 1964 ended with a hung jury when a witness confessed on the stand that he, not Mitchell, had killed the woman.

In early 1966, Governor Nelson D. Rockefeller of New York commuted the death sentence of two men, Anthony Portelli and Jerome Rosenberg, after a witness said police had tortured him to make him testify against Portelli. The men had been convicted of slaying two police detectives.

Despite public indignation over police misbehavior, many people were reluctant to put strict controls on police. The 1960s was a time of upheaval for the country: President John F. Kennedy was assassinated in Dallas in 1963; the crime rate continued to climb; violence in the inner cities was on the rise. According to Federal Bureau of Investigation figures, bank robberies rose 248 percent from 1960 to 1967. In five years, from 1962 to 1967, the number of gun assaults increased 84 percent.[15] Murders were front-page news. On television, the bloody images of crime victims were played before an increasingly fearful American public.

Against this backdrop of fear, attempts to guarantee rights to crime suspects met with anger and resentment. People charged that the courts and liberal "do-gooders" were trying to handcuff police and coddle criminals.

The same *New York Times* edition that carried a call for a behavior code for police featured a page 1 critique of the suspects' rights movement by Lewis F. Powell Jr., president of the American Bar Association. He said there was "growing reason" for the belief that recent Supreme Court decisions had favored criminals at the expense of public safety. Speaking at the annual meeting of the New York State Bar Association, Powell criticized recent court rulings as making the job of law enforcement more difficult. Citing statistics on the rising crime rate, he said, "The pendulum may have swung too far in affording rights which are abused and misused by criminals."[16] Powell would be nominated to the Supreme Court by law-and-order President Richard M. Nixon in 1971.

Police and their supporters complained loudly and often that granting rights to suspects jeopardized the public. Such rules and regulations, they said, hampered the police and made it difficult for them to convict sophisticated criminals. Confessions were seen as an important tool in obtaining convictions, and police resisted attempts to limit their ability to obtain them.

Shortly after Whitmore was arrested, the Manhattan assistant DA handling the case had strong words to say on what he viewed as attempts by the court to handcuff police:

> Let me give you the perfect example of the
> importance of confessions to law enforcement.
> This, more than anything else, will prove how

unrealistic and naive the Court is. Whitmore!
The Whitmore case. Do you know that we had
every top detective on the Wylie-Hoffert murders, and they couldn't find a clue. Not a clue.
I tell you, that if that kid hadn't confessed, we
never would have caught the killer.[17]

But, of course, the Whitmore case turned out to be a "perfect
example" of the entrapment of an innocent man by misbehaving police.

CHAPTER TWO

The Due Process Revolution

It would be easy to let anyone come and crash into your home at any time and search it and see if you possibly were committing any crime, but the Constitution says that you can't do that. Of course, that makes it more difficult to convict people; but there are certain things that an ordered society must honor in the rights of individuals . . .[1]

—Chief Justice Earl Warren

One issue central to *Miranda* and other suspects' rights cases was whether the states had to abide by the Bill of Rights. One side argued that the Bill of Rights applied only to the federal government and federal cases. The other side argued that states were also governed by the Bill of Rights and that they should not be allowed to violate a suspect's basic rights. Their arguments rested on the meaning of the Fourteenth Amendment.

The framers of the Constitution wanted to make certain that the new United States federal government didn't misuse its power. In 1791, they added ten amendments to the Constitution, called the Bill of Rights, that spelled out the rights guaranteed to citizens. Among the rights cited in the document were those viewed fundamental to the newly freed nation: freedom of speech, religion, and the press; the right to bear arms; the right to an attorney and a trial by jury; the right for people to be safe in their own homes against unreasonable government searches.

They limited the powers of the federal government in the Tenth Amendment. The federal government could not claim a right unless it was listed in the Constitution. All other rights belonged to the states or to the people.

The Bill of Rights did not end the power struggle among the federal government, state, and citizen. In an 1833 Supreme Court case, *Barron v. Baltimore*, a citizen claimed the state had taken his property without paying for it, which he said violated the Fifth Amendment.

Chief Justice John Marshall, writing the opinion for the Court, ruled that the Bill of Rights applied only to the federal government, not the states. The Constitution, he wrote, "was ordained and established by the people of the United States for themselves, for their own government, and not for the government of the individual states."[2]

The Fourteenth Amendment, passed by the Congress in 1866 and ratified by the states in 1868, placed limits on the states. Section 1 of the amendment spelled out three restrictions:

- The states couldn't deny citizens the privileges guaranteed them in the Constitution.
- The states couldn't take away life, liberty, or property without "due process"; that is, a state had to follow certain procedures before it could put a citizen to death, interfere with his or her liberty, or take away his or her property. This is known as the "due process clause."
- The states had to treat people equally.

In arguing for passage of the Fourteenth Amendment, Senator Jacob Howard of Michigan said its purpose was to protect citizens' rights against states' power. "The great object of the first section of this amendment is, therefore, to restrain the power of the states and compel them at all times to respect these fundamental rights."[3]

The first section of the Fourteenth Amendment banned states from interfering with a person's "privileges or immunities" as citizens and from taking away life, liberty, or property without due process. But it did not specifically mention the Bill of Rights.

The Supreme Court continued to rule in favor of states that argued the Bill of Rights did not apply to them. In the first case to comment on the Fourteenth Amendment, Justice Samuel F. Miller wrote that the amendment banned states from interfering with citizens' rights only when they were dealing with the federal government. For example, the states could not interfere with a citizen's right to vote in a federal election.

The justices who disagreed with the decision complained that the ruling turned the first section of the Fourteenth Amendment into "a vain and idle enactment which accomplished nothing."[4] Justice Noah Haynes Swayne wrote that "ample protection was given against oppression by the Union, but little was given against wrong and oppression by the States. That was what was intended to be supplied by this Amendment."[5]

In the 1925 case of *Gitlow v. New York*, the Supreme Court for the first time ruled that some of the rights mentioned in the Bill of Rights were protected from state, as well as federal, interference. The opinion read, in part, "we may and do assume that freedom of speech and of the press—which are protected by the First Amendment from abridgment by Congress—are among the fundamental personal rights and 'liberties' protected by the due process clause of the Fourteenth Amendment from impairment by the States."[6]

Later Court decisions added other rights mentioned in the Bill of Rights to those that the states were required to honor. But the Supreme Court has never issued a ruling that would apply the entire Bill of Rights to the states.

The Supreme Court headed by Chief Justice Earl Warren from 1953 to 1969 expanded the rights that applied to the states more than any other Court. Two of the Court's members, Justice Hugo L. Black and Justice Felix Frankfurter, argued the two sides of the issue.

Black, who served on the Court from 1937 to 1971, firmly believed that all the rights in the Bill of Rights should apply to the states. In Black's dissent in a 1948 case, he argued that it should not be up to the Court to decide which parts of the Bill of Rights should be included in state laws. He wrote, "I believe the original purpose of the Fourteenth Amendment [was] to extend to all the people of the nation the complete protection of the Bill of Rights."[7]

Frankfurter, who served on the Court from 1939 to 1962, disagreed

Justice Felix Frankfurter

with Black's view. He argued that if such a view were followed, it would "tear up by the roots much of the fabric of law in the several States."[8] States, he believed, should be able to experiment with law enforcement techniques and to respond to new problems that had not arisen in 1791 when the Bill of Rights was written. He believed that if an offense by a state "shocks the conscience" of the Court, then it should not be allowed. Otherwise, he believed, it was up to the states to run their own affairs. This case-by-case approach to the issue protected states' rights against a powerful federal government, Frankfurter believed.

After concentrating on civil rights in the 1950s, the Warren Court began to shift its focus to the criminal arena in the 1960s. One of the first major rulings in this area came in 1961 with the *Mapp v. Ohio* case.

Dollree Mapp, a twenty-eight-year-old resident of Cleveland, Ohio, was a friend of a man on the run. Police were looking for him in connection with a bombing when they knocked on Mapp's door the morning of May 23, 1957. She told them he wasn't there. When they asked if they could come in, she demanded to see a search warrant. They left, but waited outside her house.

After several hours, the police forced their way in and searched Mapp's home. They claimed they had a search warrant. During the search, police found a couple of photographs, a pencil doodle, and four pamphlets that they termed "lewd and lascivious." Mapp said the materials belonged to a former boarder at the house.

She was charged with possession of obscene materials, a violation of Ohio state law. At her trial, police never produced any evidence to show that they actually had a search warrant to enter Mapp's home. The federal and most state constitutions, including Ohio's, require that police have a valid search warrant before they search a citizen's home, business, or

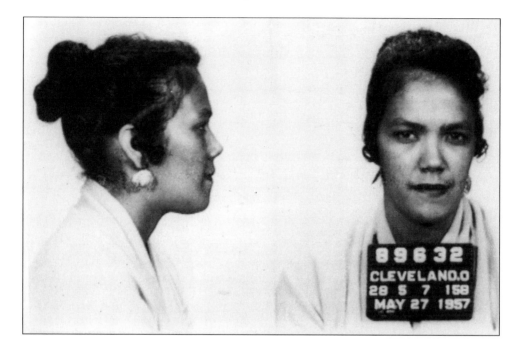

Dollree Mapp poses in police photos taken after her arrest on a charge of possessing obscene materials.

person. To obtain a warrant, police must present evidence linking the search to a crime. The warrant must describe where the search is to take place and the items to be searched for.

Mapp was convicted and sentenced to jail for up to seven years.

In hearing her appeal of the conviction, the Ohio Supreme Court ruled that the search of Mapp's home and seizure of materials had been illegal. But the court said that the evidence found in the home, even though it was collected illegally, could be used at the trial. The court upheld Mapp's conviction.

The Supreme Court agreed with the Ohio Supreme Court that Ohio police had unlawfully searched Mapp's house. But the High Court overruled Mapp's conviction. It ordered that because the police broke the rules—searched without a valid warrant—they couldn't use any of the evidence during the trial.

Not allowing evidence that was illegally obtained—called the exclusionary rule—had been used for years in federal trials. *Mapp* was a landmark case because it was the first time the Court had extended the rule to state trials.

The Court based its decision on the Fourth Amendment, which guarantees freedom against unreasonable searches, and on the Fourteenth Amendment's provision that no state can "deprive any person of life, liberty, or property, without due process of law."

The ruling marked the beginning of what many termed the "due process revolution." It was a revolution fought in the Court and in the Congress, spearheaded by a series of Court rulings that used the due process clause to require states to grant suspects the rights guaranteed in the Bill of Rights.

The revolution would peak with *Miranda v. Arizona*, a decision that would take the Court to the center of a controversy affecting the political future of the country and threatening the power of the Court itself.

CHAPTER THREE

Taking the Fifth

A system of criminal law enforcement which comes to depend on the "confession" will, in the long run, be less reliable and more subject to abuses than a system which depends on . . . evidence independently secured through skillful investigation.[1]

—Justice Arthur Goldberg
Escobedo v. Illinois

Reaction to the *Mapp* decision was mixed. In 1961, about half the states had their own exclusionary rules. The decision had little effect on the way they ran trials. For the other states, though, the ruling meant they could no longer use in court any evidence that was seized illegally. They protested that the ruling would allow criminals to go free.

Those who promoted civil liberties, however, applauded the ruling. They said it would help protect citizens from police abuse.

Supporters of states' rights objected to *Mapp* on the grounds that the

Supreme Court shouldn't be telling the states how to run their law enforcement systems. Until *Mapp*, the Court had not interfered with states' law enforcement practices unless police procedures were seen as fundamentally unfair.

For example, in 1923, the Court had reversed the state conviction of five black men charged with murdering a white man in Arkansas. The trial had been held in 45 minutes while a white mob waited outside. The jury reached a verdict in five minutes. In overturning the conviction, the Court ruled for the first time that the state court had violated the defendants' due process.

But in 1937, the Court refused to make the states abide by the Fifth Amendment's guarantee against double jeopardy. The amendment says that no one should be tried twice for the same crime.

In the 1937 case, a man named Frank Palko had been convicted of second-degree murder, but at a second trial in the same case, he was convicted of first-degree murder and sentenced to death. The Court ruled that states, as well as the federal government, had to honor "fundamental" rights. But the Court said the right against double jeopardy wasn't fundamental. The justices turned down Palko's request, and he was executed.

The Court's decision in *Palko v. Connecticut* presented a problem for lower court judges. They didn't know which rights would be considered fundamental by the Court. Under this system, the Supreme Court soon found itself dealing with the question of rights on a case-by-case basis.

From 1923 to 1960 the Court heard several hundred cases in which states were accused of violating due process. Many others, however, were requested to be heard, but the Court did not have time to review each case. Instead, the Court decided it must lay down broad, clear rules that the states could follow. The *Mapp* case was one of the first to do that, applying the Fourth Amendment to the states.

Soon the Court was asked to rule on other rights guaranteed in the Bill of Rights. In a landmark 1963 case, *Gideon v. Wainwright*, the Supreme Court ruled that defendants were guaranteed the right to an attorney to defend them at trial. Poor people charged with serious crimes had been provided attorneys at federal trials for years. But *Gideon* required states, as well, to provide lawyers for those who could not afford them. The Sixth Amendment's guarantee to the assistance of an attorney would apply to the states.

Several cases arose dealing with confessions. The Fifth Amendment guarantees that people have the right not to be forced to testify against themselves. That is why defendants and witnesses who refuse to talk at a trial say they are "taking the Fifth."

The Fifth Amendment bans the use of torture to obtain a confession. In a 1936 case the Court overturned a state conviction of two black men who had been beaten by Mississippi police with metal-studded belts until they confessed. Physical abuse, however, is not the only method police have used to get confessions. Suspects have been deprived of sleep and food; they have been questioned for days at a time. In some cases, police have threatened to arrest loved ones or promised good deals if the suspect confesses.

There are two problems with forced confessions, according to Jethro Lieberman in his book on famous Supreme Court cases. One, as in the case of Whitmore, is that the confession may not be true. "Coercion is not guaranteed to yield the truth," writes Lieberman. It only guarantees that the victim will say what the questioner wants to hear.[2]

The second concern over forced confessions is that it violates civilized behavior on which the nation was based. Forced confessions cannot be allowed, Justice Frankfurter said in a 1961 case, "because the methods used to extract them offend an underlying principle in the enforcement of our criminal law: that ours is a . . . system in which the State must establish guilt by evidence independently and freely secured and may not by coercion prove its charge against an accused out of his own mouth."[3]

In two earlier federal cases, *Mallory v. United States* and *McNabb v. United States*, the Court had ruled that suspects must be arraigned promptly. If they were not, any confessions made during the time before arraignment could not be used in court. That gave police less time to interrogate suspects. In its 1968 Omnibus Crime Control and Safe Streets Act, Congress allowed police to spend up to six hours with a suspect before arraignment.

In 1964 a state case, *Malloy v. Hogan*, gave the Court the chance to rule on the Fifth Amendment's guarantees as they affected states. By the 1960s, all 50 states had laws against forced confessions. But the Court continued to be asked to decide which confessions were forced. In *Malloy*, the Court overruled a state court that sent a man to jail when he refused to testify against himself during a police investigation that involved gambling. The ruling said states must abide by the Fifth Amendment and not force defendants to testify against themselves. It gave state court judges national guidelines to follow when deciding whether a defendant could claim the Fifth. The Fifth won't apply, the Court said, only when it can be shown that the defendant's statements "cannot possibly have . . . a tendency to incriminate."[4]

In 1964, the Court ruled on two cases that would set the stage for the *Miranda* decision. The first, a federal case, involved Winston Massiah, a merchant seaman. Massiah and several of his shipmates were arrested and charged with possessing narcotics aboard a United States vessel. The defendants were released on bail, and Massiah hired a lawyer to represent him. One of the seamen agreed to help the police. He allowed his car to be bugged and tricked Massiah into making incriminating statements. The agents told the jury of the conversations at Massiah's trial, and he was convicted.

The Supreme Court, on a 6 to 3 vote, overturned Massiah's conviction. The Court said the agents had violated Massiah's Sixth Amendment rights to have his attorney with him during questioning. "In all criminal prosecutions," wrote Justice Potter Stewart in the majority opinion, "the accused shall enjoy the right . . . to have the assistance of counsel for his defense."[5]

Justice Byron R. White, joined by Justices Tom C. Clark and John Marshall Harlan, disagreed. He charged in his dissent, "This is nothing more than a thinly disguised constitutional policy of minimizing or entirely prohibiting the use in evidence of voluntary out-of-court admissions and confessions made by the accused."[6]

States' rights wasn't an issue because *Massiah* was a federal case. But *Massiah* laid the groundwork for *Miranda* by ruling that confessions, even voluntary ones, could be thrown out of court if police interfered with the defendant's right to a lawyer.

Danny Escobedo, a Chicago laborer, played the lead role in the second case that would bring the Court closer to the *Miranda* ruling. Escobedo's brother-in-law was shot and killed on the night of January 19, 1960. The next morning, police arrested Escobedo, took him to the station house, and questioned him about the murder. He made no statement, and at 5 P.M. he was released on a court order obtained by his lawyer.

On the evening of January 30, the police arrested Escobedo and his

38 Danny Escobedo, right, confers with Ralph C. Hartsough Jr., a lawyer, in municipal court in Chicago.

sister, who had been married to the man who was killed. During the ride to the station, police told Escobedo that another man involved in the murder had told them Escobedo had done it. At that point, Escobedo asked to see his lawyer. The police denied his request.

Shortly after Escobedo arrived at the station, his lawyer appeared. Police told the lawyer he couldn't see his client until after Escobedo had been questioned.

For the next three hours, police interrogated Escobedo about the murder. The twenty-two-year-old, who had no previous police record, was handcuffed and made to stand while police questioned him. At one point, they brought in the man who had accused Escobedo of being the gunman. Escobedo told him he was lying and said, "I didn't shoot Manuel, you did it."[7]

After that, he made other statements linking himself to the murder. At the end of the session, the assistant state's attorney convinced Escobedo to make a statement on the case. No one told Escobedo of his right to remain silent. Throughout the night, Escobedo had told police he wanted to see his lawyer. The lawyer had also demanded to see his client.

At his trial, Escobedo's statements were read to the jury, which convicted him. He appealed. The Supreme Court overturned his conviction, ruling that police had unlawfully denied Escobedo his Sixth Amendment right to an attorney. If he had consulted with his lawyer, the Court reasoned, the lawyer would have told Escobedo of his right to remain silent. Therefore, his statements could not be used against him in court.

Gideon had confirmed the right of defendants to be represented by a lawyer during a trial. But the *Escobedo* ruling was the first time the Court had extended that right to the police station. Justice Arthur Goldberg, in his majority opinion, noted the importance of allowing suspects to consult with their attorneys before they were questioned by police. "The right to use counsel at the formal trial [would be] a very hollow thing [if], for all practical purposes, the conviction is already assured by pretrial examination."[8]

Justices Harlan, White, Clark, and Stewart objected bitterly to the opinion. In his dissent, Harlan called it "ill-conceived" and said it "seriously and unjustifiably fetters perfectly legitimate methods of criminal law enforcement."[9] White charged that the right to counsel, according to the *Escobedo* ruling, not only entitled the accused to a lawyer's help in preparing a case for trial but also stood "as an impenetrable barrier to any interrogation once the accused has become a suspect."[10]

Despite the dissenting justices' alarm, few cases fit the circumstances outlined in *Escobedo*. Most courts ruled that suspects taken into police custody were entitled to lawyers only when they asked for them, as Escobedo had done. In most cases, though, suspects didn't ask for lawyers until after they were accused of a crime. That often came after police questioning and after a suspect had already confessed.

Most confession cases coming before the Supreme Court involved not the question of whether a suspect had a lawyer, but whether his or her confession had been voluntary. Between 1954 and 1966, the Supreme Court issued 36 opinions on whether confessions were voluntary. In deciding the cases, the justices used what was called the "totality of circumstances." That meant they studied everything about the confession: the suspect's age, mental ability, level of education; the length and time of questioning; the number of police involved. If the circumstances, added together, put unfair pressure on the suspect, then the Court ruled in his or her favor. The justices rejected the claims of those who had only a few of the factors working against them.

One problem with that approach, however, was that there was no firm guideline on which circumstances, or how many, resulted in an involuntary confession. Some Supreme Court rulings allowed confessions to be used in court. Other decisions threw them out. There didn't seem to be much difference between the two types of cases.

Judges in lower courts had no way of knowing how the Court would rule on a particular case. During the early 1960s, Texas courts upheld several convictions that involved suspects who claimed they were forced to confess. One had been beaten, another had been questioned for three days, and a third had been described as having the mental abilities of a three- to six-year-old.

State courts, it seemed, could find a Supreme Court decision on confessions that would justify almost any ruling. Many believed it was time for the Court to set the record straight.

CHAPTER FOUR

The Cases

We can have the Constitution, the best laws in the land, and the most honest reviews by courts—but unless the law enforcement profession is steeped in the democratic tradition, maintains the highest in ethics, and makes its work a career of honor, civil liberties will continually—and without end— be violated.[1]

—J. Edgar Hoover
Director of the FBI, 1924-1972

Ernesto Miranda was asleep when police knocked on his door the morning of March 13, 1963, and demanded he go with them to the police station in Phoenix, Arizona. Miranda, twenty-three, was familiar with the place. In 1962 he had been arrested for robbing a Phoenix bank employee of $8. A drifter who occasionally worked as a trucker's helper, Miranda had dropped out of school before finishing the ninth grade.

Ernesto Miranda under arrest

In a 1973 interview, Miranda said, "I didn't know whether I had a choice [about going to the police station]. They said they couldn't tell me anything. Once we got there, they started interrogating me about a kidnap case, telling me that they weren't sure that I had committed the crime or not, but that they had certain information and wanted to get it straightened out."[2]

Miranda stood in a lineup with several other men. The victim, an eighteen-year-old woman who worked at a local theater, pointed at him. He was the man, she said, who had kidnapped her, driven her into the desert, and raped her ten days before.

The police took Miranda to a separate room to question him about the crime. At first, he said he knew nothing about the crime. After two hours of questioning by the police, he confessed. At 1:30 P.M. Miranda wrote out his confession and details about the crime.

In the 1973 interview, he said the police told him the victim had identified him and that he "might as well admit to the crime."[3]

Miranda was arrested and put in jail. He had no lawyer with him at the police station or at a preliminary hearing. At the arraignment, where he was formally charged with the crimes, the judge appointed a lawyer to represent him. Miranda's lawyer—a seventy-three-year-old man named Alvin Moore—had practiced little criminal law for the past 16 years.

Because Miranda had confessed, the lawyer advised him to plead guilty. Miranda refused but agreed to plead guilty by reason of insanity. Before his trial, a psychiatrist examined Miranda. The doctor reported that Miranda had had mental problems since he was a child. He had been arrested for being a Peeping Tom, had been picked up for attempted rape when he was fifteen, and had been dishonorably discharged from the army. According to the doctor, Miranda was immature, with no control over his impulses. But Miranda was not insane, the doctor said, and he knew the difference between right and wrong.

Miranda's lawyer raised the point that his client had not been told of his right to consult with an attorney during police questioning. Because of this oversight, his lawyer argued, Miranda's confession should not be used in court.

In his instructions to the jury, the judge commented on Miranda's lack of an attorney during questioning:

> The fact that the defendant was under arrest at
> the time he made a confession, that he was not
> at the time represented by Counsel, that he was
> not told that any statements he might make
> could or would be used against him, in and of
> themselves, will not render [his] confession
> involuntary.[4]

The jury found Miranda guilty of kidnapping and rape. He was sentenced to 20 to 30 years in jail. Miranda appealed his conviction. A new lawyer, John J. Flynn of Phoenix, agreed to represent him. The case was heard in Arizona Supreme Court in 1965. The court ruled that Miranda's rights were not violated by the lower court's ruling that his confession could be used against him. Miranda decided to take his case to the Supreme Court of the United States.

The Supreme Court is the highest court in the country. Its decision on a case is the final word. The Supreme Court decides issues that can affect every person in the nation. It has decided cases on slavery, abortion, school segregation, and many other important issues.

People wait outside the Supreme Court building in Washington, D.C. They hope to attend a hearing conducted by the Supreme Court justices.

Each year the Court receives thousands of requests to hear cases. Most of them have been tried in lower courts and appealed. The nine-member Court hears only a small portion of them.

The Court's term runs from October to late June or early July. At the beginning of its session, the justices review cases and pick the ones they will hear. Most people seeking a decision from the Court submit a petition for certiorari. Certiorari means that the case will be moved from a lower court to a higher court for review. The petition outlines the case and gives reasons why the Court should review it. Most petitions for certiorari are typed and prepared by lawyers. Others are handwritten by prisoners who want the Court to overturn their convictions. They can range from a few paragraphs to many pages long.

The justices gather in a private conference room to discuss the cases. Since no one else is allowed in the room, the newest justice acts as errand boy (or girl). He or she must carry messages and requests from the justices to the staff outside.

The justices work from a list of cases the chief justice considers important. After a brief review of each case, the justices go around the table. The justices who have served on the Court longest speak first. After everyone has commented on the case, the justices vote on whether to hear it. Four justices must vote to consider the case in order for it to come before the Court.

To win a spot on the Court's docket, a case must involve one of three issues. It must deal with constitutional rights or questions, rulings by different courts that conflict with each other, or a decision by a state court on a federal law.

Once a case is selected, lawyers for both sides must submit briefs. Briefs are the legal documents in which lawyers argue their cases. In the briefs the lawyers discuss the facts of the case. They cite laws that support their case and answer charges made by lawyers for the other side. The judges read the briefs to help them decide the case.

After the *Escobedo* ruling in June 1964, the Supreme Court was flooded with cases dealing with confessions. The court clerk set them aside to await the justices' decision on what to do about the issue. Each was marked "E.C.," meaning *Escobedo* case. About 140 of the confessions cases had been received by November 1965.[5] The Supreme Court justices decided they must rule, once and for all, on the issue.

They picked four from the pile of E.C. cases. Because Miranda's case was listed first, the decision eventually issued by the Court became known as *Miranda v. Arizona*. Also selected for hearing were *Vignera v. New York*, *Westover v. United States*, and *Johnson v. New Jersey*. *California v. Stewart* was added to the list later.

Vignera v. New York involved the case of Michael Vignera. On October 14, 1960, Vignera had been picked up by New York City police in connection with a dress shop robbery. The owner identified Vignera as the man who had robbed her of cash, travelers' checks, and credit cards three days earlier. Police arrested Vignera at 3 P.M. Under questioning by police, Vignera admitted that he had used a toy gun in the robbery and had taken about $93 from the shop.

Later that night, Vignera was taken to the 70th Precinct in Brooklyn. After 11 P.M., an assistant DA questioned him and he confessed again. The confession was recorded. It was not until the next day that Vignera, who had been held in jail, was finally arraigned. On his way to court, in response to more questions from police, he admitted he had used a knife, not a gun, in the robbery.

During Vignera's trial, in which his confession was used, his attorney asked police whether he had been told of his right to counsel. The judge ruled that the police did not have to answer that question. The jury found Vignera guilty of first-degree robbery and sentenced him to 30 to 60 years in jail. In his brief for the appeal of the case, the district attorney noted that Vignera had not been warned of his right to an attorney.

Sylvester Johnson and Stanley Cassidy, the petitioners in *Johnson v. New Jersey*, had been arrested for a murder that occurred during a robbery in Camden, New Jersey, on January 24, 1958. Five days after the murder, at 4 A.M., seven police officers arrived at the home of Cassidy. He was high on marijuana. Police asked him to come to the police station to talk about the robbery.

Five hours later, Cassidy, who had never been arrested or interrogated by police before, confessed to the robbery. Before the confession was recorded, the police chief warned Cassidy "that everything you tell me must be of your own free will." He also told Cassidy that anything he said could be used against him. Cassidy, twenty-five, was not told of his right to an attorney. He was held and interrogated for three days before being taken to court for arraignment.

Johnson, twenty-one, with a seventh-grade education, was arrested in the late afternoon of January 29. He was interrogated that evening and the following day. Police denied his request to see his family and his lawyer. He was given the same warning that Cassidy had been given. At 6:15 P.M. on January 30 he confessed to the robbery. Both Johnson and Cassidy were found guilty and sentenced to death. Their appeals were denied by the appeals court and the New Jersey Supreme Court. The conviction of a third defendant, Wayne Godfrey, was overturned because the court ruled he had been forced to confess. At a new trial, he was sentenced to life in prison.

California v. Stewart involved a series of robberies that occurred in

Los Angeles between December 21, 1962, and January 30, 1963. A woman was murdered during one of the robberies. Police went to Roy Allen Stewart's house on January 31 to arrest him in the crimes. During a search of the house, police found various items belonging to the robbery victims. They arrested all five people who were in the house at the time, including Stewart.

Over the next five days, police interrogated Stewart eight times. During the ninth interrogation session, he confessed to the robbery in which the victim had died. The others arrested in the case were released. Stewart did not ask to see an attorney, and the police did not tell him of his right to consult one. Nor did the police advise him of his right to remain silent.

A jury found Stewart guilty of robbery and murder, and he was sentenced to death. On appeal, the California Supreme Court overturned his conviction because he had not been told of his right to an attorney. The court based its ruling on the *Escobedo* case. The state of California appealed the decision to the U.S. Supreme Court.

In the only federal case, *Westover v. United States*, Carl Calvin Westover had been arrested on March 20, 1963, for two Kansas City, Missouri, robberies. After 14 hours of questioning by the local police, he was turned over to the Federal Bureau of Investigation. The FBI was investigating two bank robberies they believed Westover had committed in California.

Westover, who denied he was connected to the two local robberies, was not told of his rights by the Kansas City police. The FBI agents, however, told Westover he could remain silent, that if he said anything it could be used against him, and that he had the right to consult an attorney. After two hours with the FBI, Westover confessed to the two California robberies. He was found guilty and sentenced to 15 years on each count.

Westover's lawyer asked the Court to decide whether his client's right to counsel and right not to incriminate himself had been denied. He noted that Westover's confession had come only after 15 to 17 hours of questioning in a "joint effort" between the state and the federal government.

All five cases were scheduled for oral arguments on February 28, 1966. By the time of the Supreme Court hearing, lawyers had filed 14 briefs in the cases. The briefs filled 700 pages.[6]

Among those filing briefs in the cases were lawyers representing each of the convicted men. The states of Arizona, New York, New Jersey, and California—where five of the six men were convicted—also filed briefs. In *Westover v. United States*, a federal case, attorneys for the United States filed a brief.

In many cases, groups that agree with one side or the other may want to offer their views on the issue. These groups are called amicus curiae, meaning "friend of the court." Lawyers from these groups file their views in briefs submitted to the Court. In some cases, the Court allows them to testify during oral arguments.

Several groups filed amicus briefs in the *Miranda* cases. The National District Attorneys Association and the attorneys general of 27 states argued for the states' position that suspects have no right to an attorney before being arraigned. The American Civil Liberties Union also submitted briefs in the cases. The group argued on the side of the convicted men, supporting their right not to be forced to incriminate themselves.

CHAPTER FIVE

The Arguments

*I suppose that even in an extreme
state, those people who are convicted
of crime are really guilty, but I,
equally, suppose that you will join me
in finding it abhorrent if those people
were convicted without having counsel
in what we consider to be a fair trial.*[1]

—Justice Abe Fortas
Oral arguments, *Vignera v. New York*

February 28, 1966, was rainy and mild, nearing the
end of winter in Washington, D.C. A crowd of lawyers made their way up
the marble steps of the Supreme Court building. Above the huge marble
columns in front of the building, the motto, "Equal Justice Under Law,"
proclaims the Court's mission. To the right of the steps, a statue of a man
representing law greeted those who passed; to the left, the stone figure of
a seated woman represented justice.

The courtroom where Supreme Court justices hear cases

Opening the heavy oak door, the lawyers stepped inside the court-room. For those who had not been inside this room before, it was an awe-inspiring experience. Surrounding the room were 24 columns of Italian marble. Standing on red carpet, the lawyers viewed the red velvet curtains through which the justices would soon emerge.

"Oyez, oyez, oyez!" the bailiff called, an ancient term meaning "hear ye." Everyone in the courtroom stood. The nine, black-robed justices entered and sat in the black leather chairs facing the room.

Chief Justice Earl Warren sat in the center of the nine justices. He had been appointed to the Court in 1954. As a district attorney and attorney general of California, Warren earned a reputation as a crime fighter. A former governor of California, Warren was nominated by President Dwight D. Eisenhower, who later called the nomination "the biggest damn-fool mistake I ever made."[2]

To Warren's right sat Hugo L. Black, the justice who had served the longest on the Court. Appointed to the Court in 1937, Black had gained fame while a public prosecutor in Alabama for his investigation of police brutality while questioning suspects. He served as a U.S. senator before being nominated to the Court by President Franklin D. Roosevelt.

William O. Douglas, the second most senior justice, sat to the left of Warren. Douglas taught at Columbia and Yale Law Schools and served as chair of the Securities and Exchange Commission before his appointment to the Court in 1939. He, too, was nominated by Roosevelt.

Beside Douglas sat John Marshall Harlan, nominated to the Court in 1955 by Eisenhower. He had served as assistant U.S. attorney, special assistant to the attorney general of New York, and on the U.S. Court of Appeals. He was named for his grandfather, Supreme Court Justice John Marshall Harlan, who served on the Court from 1877 to 1911.

On Harlan's left was Potter Stewart. He had worked briefly as a Wall Street lawyer and had served on the Sixth Circuit Court of Appeals. An Eisenhower nominee, he was appointed to the Court in 1959.

Abe Fortas, the newest member on the Court, sat next to Stewart. Fortas, nominated by President Lyndon B. Johnson and appointed in 1965, had argued the *Gideon* case before the Court in 1963 as the lawyer for the defense.

On Black's right sat Clark. He had worked at his father's law firm in Texas, then taken jobs as a district attorney in Dallas County. He held several posts in President Harry S Truman's administration, serving as U.S. attorney general from 1945 to 1949, when Truman appointed him to the Supreme Court.

Next to Clark was William Joseph Brennan Jr., an Eisenhower nominee appointed to the Court in 1956. Brennan served as a New Jersey Superior Court judge and as an associate judge on the state supreme court before being named to the High Court.

Byron R. White, one of only two justices nominated by President John F. Kennedy, sat next to Brennan. White had served as deputy U.S. attorney general in Kennedy's Administration before his appointment in 1962.

The lawyers in the *Miranda* case took their seats at the benches opposite the justices. Those who would argue in the other cases sat in chairs along the side, awaiting their turn to speak. A clock hanging from the ceiling above the justices reminded the lawyers that they would have only one-half hour each to argue their cases.

Miranda, who was in jail, did not attend the hearing. He would depend on his lawyer to speak for him.

The arguments would revolve around three basic issues:

- **Public safety.** The rights of suspects must be balanced against the rights of the public to be secure. The Court should not interfere with police officers' ability to do their job. This position was argued most vigorously by the National District Attorneys Association.

- **Rights of the people.** The Constitution and the Bill of Rights protect the rights of all. The society must operate under the rule of law. Police cannot be allowed to violate people's rights. Lawyers are needed to tell people about their rights, since people can't be protected if they don't know what their rights are. This position was argued by lawyers who represented the convicted men and by the American Civil Liberties Union.

- **States' rights.** It is up to the states to oversee their own law enforcement systems. The Court should have a say only in federal cases. This position was argued by the lawyer representing the attorneys general of 27 states.

John J. Flynn, representing Miranda, spoke first. He outlined the facts of the case, then described Miranda's confession. Miranda had written his confession on a form that contained a typed statement:

I, Ernesto A. Miranda, do hereby swear that I
make this statement voluntarily and of my own
free will, with no threats, coercion or promises
of immunity and with full knowledge of my
legal rights, understanding any statement I
make may be used against me.[3]

In denying his appeal, the Arizona Supreme Court had ruled that the
typed warning alerted Miranda to his rights. The court also noted that
Miranda had not asked for a lawyer. Therefore, it ruled, the police had not
denied his request or violated his right to an attorney, as they had in the
Escobedo case.

Flynn argued that police had not told his client he had the right to
remain silent or that he could consult with an attorney. An educated, rich
man might have known his rights, Flynn said. But Miranda didn't have
these advantages. He should have been told of his rights when he first came
into police custody, Flynn argued.

Under the facts and circumstances in Miranda
of a man of limited education, of a man who
certainly is mentally abnormal, who is, certainly, an indigent, police at the very least had
an obligation to extend to this man, not only his
clear 5th Amendment right, but to accord him
the right of counsel.[4]

Without a lawyer to advise him, Flynn noted, a suspect might not
understand or know about the rights guaranteed him by the Fifth Amend-

ment. If that were the case, the suspect couldn't take advantage of his rights.

> He is at the very least entitled . . . to be repre-
> sented by counsel and to be advised by counsel
> of his rights under the 5th Amendment of the
> Constitution, or he has no such right.[5]

Justice Stewart asked what a suspect's rights were during interrogation. Flynn replied they included "the right not to incriminate himself . . . a right to be free from further questioning by the police department . . . the right at the ultimate time to be represented adequately by counsel, and. . . if he was too poor to employ counsel, the state would furnish him counsel."[6]

Responding to a question posed by Justice Fortas, Flynn noted that a lawyer could do little to help Miranda once he made his confession. Miranda most needed the help of a lawyer during questioning, before he confessed, Flynn said.

> After the two-hour interrogation, the mere
> formality of supplying counsel to Ernest
> Miranda at the time of trial . . . would be
> nothing more than a mockery of his 6th
> Amendment right to be represented in court.[7]

Flynn agreed that Miranda had not been forced to confess through threats or promises. But, he argued, he was compelled to confess, "not by gunpoint," but because he did not know he had the right to remain silent.

Justice Black asked if Miranda might have felt compelled to confess because he was being held in custody by the police. "Control and custody—why would that not tend to show some kind of coercion?"[8]

Flynn agreed, noting that a suspect might also believe he had to confess because he had been raised to tell the truth and respect authority.

Flynn's time for argument was over. Gary K. Nelson, assistant attorney general, rose to present the state of Arizona's case. He said the police had told Miranda of his rights, though it wasn't clear when the warning had been given.

In answer to a question by Justice Fortas, Nelson said that if a warning was needed, it would have to be given before the suspect said anything to be effective. "I would think that to be of any effect, it [the warning] must be given before he made any statements."[9]

Upon further questioning by Fortas, Nelson argued that warnings were not needed in every case. The Court, he said, should look at all the circumstances and then decide whether a warning was needed. In making a decision, Nelson said, the Court should consider the suspect's "age, his experience, his background, the type of questioning, the length of questioning, the time of day perhaps—all of these factors."[10]

For years the Court had looked at the circumstances of a case to determine whether a confession was voluntary.

Nelson contended that Miranda had not needed a warning of his rights. The police had given him a warning anyway, he said, of "every warning, except the right . . . to counsel. . . . The only possible thing that happened to Mr. Miranda . . . assuming that he had the capability of understanding it all, is the fact that he did not get the specific warning of his right to counsel."[11]

Nelson told the justices that if all suspects had to have a lawyer or had to say they didn't want a lawyer before confessing, "a serious problem in the enforcement of our criminal law will occur."[12]

Once suspects have lawyers with them, Nelson said, "interrogation ceases immediately." The lawyer would first have to talk with the suspect to learn about the case. Then the lawyer might have to study the case against the suspect. Finally, said Nelson, the lawyer would advise the suspect not to say anything.[13]

Justice Black asked if that wasn't the object of the Fifth Amendment. "Is there any difference," he asked Nelson, "what the lawyer tells him and what the Fifth Amendment tells him?"[14]

Nelson agreed that both were the same. But, he argued, questioning was important to both police and suspect. In some cases, he said, the suspect could prove he was not guilty by answering police questions. If a suspect refused to answer after being warned of his rights, police might be even more convinced of his guilt, Nelson said.

Telford Taylor, who presented the case for the attorneys general of 27 states, took his turn before the Court. Arguing on the side of Arizona, he said a suspect did not have to have a lawyer or waive his right for a lawyer for a confession to be valid. Taylor said, "The Fifth Amendment cannot and should not be read as requiring counsel to be present at the time the confession is taken."[15]

Taylor said state legislatures and not the Court should decide whether suspects should be warned of their rights in state cases. He noted that when the *Gideon* case was decided, most of the states had already adopted laws requiring lawyers be provided for poor people. A similar situation occurred in *Mapp*, with about half the states already using the exclusionary rule. Taylor agreed that every state had laws against forcing people to testify against themselves. But none, he said, required suspects to be told

Justice Hugo L. Black

of their rights to remain silent and to an attorney before police questioning. "I don't know a single state that presently excludes confessions that are taken pre-arraignment in the absence of counsel,"[15] Taylor told the Court.

Miranda, it was noted, had not asked for an attorney as Escobedo had. Justice Fortas asked if it were not "too late in the day" to allow an attorney only to those who asked for one.[17]

Duane R. Nedrud, acting for the National District Attorneys Association, spoke next. The DA group had filed an amicus brief in the case on behalf of the state of Arizona. He talked about two competing needs of society: the rights of suspects versus the right of the public to be protected from crime.

To limit the use of confessions, he said, would take "from the police a most important piece of evidence." A suspect who asks for a lawyer should have one, Nedrud said, but "I do not think that we should in effect encourage him to have a lawyer."[18]

To that, Chief Justice Warren asked, "Why do you say we should not encourage him to have a lawyer? Are lawyers a menace?"[19] That elicited smiles from the audience.

Nedrud, a lawyer himself, chose not to use the word *menace*. Instead, he said a lawyer would "prevent a confession from being obtained."[20] He argued that suspects aren't entitled to lawyers until they go to trial.

Justice Douglas pointed out that "very important rights can be lost many weeks or days prior to the trial."[21]

Nedrud warned, however, that there would be fewer convictions if suspects had lawyers during police questioning.

Justice Black responded, "Can you think of any time when he needs a lawyer more than at . . . the point of detention?"[22]

Nedrud ended his presentation with a plea to the Court. "I would hope

Justice Abe Fortas

. . . that this Court . . . would . . . not go so far as to prevent the police from protecting us."[23]

Attorneys in the other four cases took their turn before the Court. Each had his own style. Some kept strictly to the facts of their particular case. Others argued for a broader interpretation that would affect the law nationally.

Victor M. Earle III, arguing for Vignera, suggested that a suspect had a right to an attorney "the moment when the state proceeded against him."[24] He proposed that police be required to issue a warning to all suspects informing them of their rights to remain silent and to an attorney.

Earle argued against using circumstances to determine whether warnings were needed. Such a measure was too vague and would result in many appeals. The Court, he noted, would not have time to review every case. "We need some specific guidelines as *Escobedo* to help [the lower courts] along the way,"[25] he told the justices.

William I. Siegel, assistant DA of Kings County, New York, spoke on behalf of the state of New York. He noted that in some cases confessions have turned out to be untrue. But, he added, law enforcement, like every other human institution, is not perfect.

Fortas said the issue of suspects' rights should be seen "in terms of the great human adventure towards some kind of truly civilized order." The Bill of Rights, he noted, was designed to eliminate the conviction of innocent people. He added that the cases before the Court dealt with more than just "the criminal in society." They also involved the "relationship of the state and the individual." A mark of civilized society, according to Fortas, is a guarantee that everyone—even the guilty—receive fair treatment.[26]

Siegel argued that a society that isn't protected from criminals will not remain civilized. "The problem that is before this Court," he told the justices, "is just how to keep the balance between the ultimate necessity of the civilized, peaceful society and the Constitutional rights of a specific defendant."[27]

Thurgood Marshall, as solicitor general of the United States, spoke for the FBI in the *Westover* case. President Lyndon Johnson would appoint Marshall to the Supreme Court the following year, in 1967. In this case, Marshall argued that it would be impossible to provide lawyers to every poor suspect brought to the police station.

Chief Justice Warren countered with an incident that had taken place in Washington, D.C. in the early 1960s. He said police had picked up 90 people and thrown them in jail because they looked like a robbery suspect. They weren't released until the next day. As it turned out, none of the 90 was guilty of the crime.

"Would you say that those who had lawyers there . . . could get out?" Warren asked. "But with the rest of them who had no lawyers and were poor . . . do you think that the police would have the right to retain them and question them?"[28]

Marshall replied that the arrest of the 90 had been illegal. Any confession under those circumstances, he said, could not have been used in court anyway.

Attorneys in the *Johnson* and *Stewart* cases argued for their clients. The hearing ended at last. Oral arguments in the *Miranda* cases had stretched over three days. Thirteen lawyers had testified for more than seven hours. The transcript, or typed record, of the hearing filled 280 pages.

Now the decision on how to ensure the rights of suspects was in the hands of the nine Supreme Court justices.

CHAPTER SIX

The Decision

No system of criminal justice can, or should, survive if it comes to depend for its continued effectiveness on the citizens' abdication through unawareness of their constitutional rights.[1]

—Justice Arthur Goldberg
Escobedo v. Illinois

Chief Justice Earl Warren delivered the *Miranda* opinion on June 13, 1966. The 5 to 4 decision overturned the convictions of Miranda, Vignera, and Westover, and upheld Stewart's reversal.

It also set specific rules governing confessions by suspects. Before police could question suspects, they would be required to warn them of their rights. Suspects would have to be told they had a right to remain silent, that any statement they made could be used against them in court, that they had a right to have an attorney with them, and that if they could not afford an attorney, one would be provided for them. Such warnings were already being given routinely by the FBI, Warren noted.

The ruling went on to say that suspects could waive their rights and

Chief Justice Earl Warren

talk with police if they chose. But the waiver had to be made "voluntarily, knowingly, and intelligently."[2] And, if suspects waived their rights but later asked for an attorney, police had to stop their questions until a lawyer was present. Likewise, police would have to stop interrogating suspects who said they did not want to answer any more questions.

Suspects' confessions or incriminating statements would be thrown out of court if the police had failed to tell them of their rights or if they had interrogated them for long periods of time. It was up to police, not defendants, to prove that confessions were given voluntarily and that defendants had waived their rights.

The ruling would still allow police to question people at a crime scene and to hold suspects at police headquarters while checking their stories. Confessions given without police questioning would also be allowed.

The 61-page decision applied to those charged with felonies or misdemeanors in both state and federal cases. Warren based his decision on the Fifth Amendment, guaranteeing the right against self-incrimination. But he also noted that the presence of an attorney, a right guaranteed by the Sixth Amendment, helped to protect a person's Fifth Amendment rights. Without an attorney, he said, a person could be intimidated into talking by police. The mere fact of being in a police station could be seen as a threat to some, Warren noted. He wrote, "Therefore, the right to have counsel present at the interrogation is indispensable to the protection of the Fifth Amendment privilege."[3]

Fifth Amendment rights are "fundamental to our system of constitutional rule,"[4] Warren wrote. He said the states, as well as the federal government, were required to honor those rights. Warren based that decision on past cases, including *Escobedo* and *Malloy*, that had already applied Fifth and Sixth Amendment rights to the states.

Warren praised police "when their services are honorably performed." But, he added, when they use unfair methods to pressure suspects into confessing, "they can become as great a menace to society as any criminal we have."[5]

The new rules were needed, Warren said, to stop police from abusing suspects. He cited a 1965 case in which New York police "beat, kicked, and placed lighted cigarette butts on the back of a potential witness."[6] Even when police did not use physical abuse, they could coerce suspects into confessing by psychological means, Warren said. He quoted several passages from police manuals that coached police in ways to convince a suspect to confess. The methods included a "Mutt and Jeff" approach, where one officer posed as the "good cop" and the other took the role of the "bad cop."

Warren used the Whitmore case as a "conspicuous example" of how interrogation methods could result in a false confession. Though the *Miranda* cases all involved men who were later found guilty of their crimes, the Whitmore case demonstrated why safeguards were necessary. The *Miranda* warning might at times protect the guilty, but it was needed to protect the innocent.

Because police questioning had traditionally occurred behind closed doors, there was no way to tell if police were treating suspects properly. Warren reasoned that suspects' rights would be safeguarded during police questioning if they had a lawyer with them.

The opinion, described as "breaking new constitutional grounds,"[7] split the Court into bitter camps. "At times the emotion in [Warren's] voice . . . bespoke the deep division in the Court over the new doctrine,"[8] the *New York Times* reported in an account of the day.

Reading their bitter dissents, the justices opposed to the *Miranda* ruling were equally emotional. Harlan's face was "flushed" and "his voice occasionally faltering with emotion" as he denounced the decision.[9] Calling it a "hazardous experimentation," Harlan said the presence of a lawyer during questioning "invites the end of the interrogation."[10]

He continued:

> We do know that some crimes cannot be solved
> without confessions, that ample expert testi-
> mony attests to their importance in crime
> control, and that the Court is taking a real risk
> with society's welfare in imposing its new
> regime on the country.[11]

White, who joined Harlan's dissent and wrote one of his own, warned the ruling would hinder the work of the police.

> In some unknown number of cases the Court's
> rule will return a killer, a rapist or other
> criminal to the streets . . . to repeat his crime
> whenever it pleases him.[12]

Justice Stewart joined in the dissents of both White and Harlan. Justice Clark wrote a separate dissent, agreeing with the Warren opinion in the *Stewart* case but disagreeing in the rest.

The dissenting justices weren't the only ones outraged by the decision. The *Miranda* ruling brought howls of protest from those in law enforcement. Claiming that confessions were the "backbone of law enforcement,"[13] police charged that the ruling would "handcuff" them in their efforts against crime. "You might as well burn up the books on the science

Justice John Marshall Harlan

of police interrogation," a Houston officer complained.[14] A Nevada police chief called *Miranda* "another shackle that the Supreme Court gives us . . . in the handling of criminal cases." He said he hoped that "some day they may give us an equal chance with the criminals."[15]

Not everyone in law enforcement was upset by *Miranda*. A spokesman for the International Association for Chiefs of Police in Washington, D.C., was quoted as saying, "This isn't so earth-shaking. Most professional police officials in this country have long felt that you should advise a suspect of his right to remain silent and to have counsel."[16]

Warren's opinion was sharply different from the usual ruling. In most cases, the Court left it up to the states to devise their own ways of making sure rulings were followed. Warren, however, had given step-by-step instructions to police on what to say to suspects. The states and police officials saw this as an intrusion by the Court into police operations. Warren's critics said it was up to state legislators, not the Court, to set up such specific guidelines.

The ACLU praised the decision as an "important buttress to the constitutional guarantee of due process of law." But the group said the ruling didn't "go far enough in protecting those who most need protection." The ACLU spokesman said the Court should have required attorneys at the police station for all suspects. Lawyers were needed, the ACLU argued, to make sure suspects voluntarily waived their rights, if they chose to do that.[17]

A week after issuing the *Miranda* decision, the Court ruled in favor of New Jersey in its case against Johnson and Cassidy. The convictions of the two men had been final long before *Escobedo* and *Miranda* had been decided. The justices used the case to decide which cases would be heard under the new *Miranda* ruling and which cases would not. The opinion, written by Warren, ruled that appeals based on *Miranda* would be heard in cases that had not yet gone to trial as of June 13, 1966—the date *Miranda* was issued. Defendants whose trials had already been held by that date would not be allowed to appeal using the issues raised in *Miranda*. Johnson and Cassidy—because their trial had been held in 1960—could not argue that police had failed to read them their rights. Black and Douglas dissented.

A rising crime rate and highly publicized violent crimes led many people to oppose suspects' rights, particularly those protected by the *Miranda* ruling. Above, New York City police patrol the scene of a shootout.

Aftermath

*Justice, though due to the accused, is
due to the accuser also. The concept of
fairness must not be strained till it is
narrowed to a filament. We are to
keep the balance true.*[1]

—Justice Benjamin N. Cardozo
Snyder v. Massachusetts

The *Johnson* decision pleased neither side of the
Miranda debate. Defendants lucky enough to have had their trials delayed
by slow-acting courts could appeal. Those in more efficient districts could
not. Proponents of suspects' rights saw this as an injustice.

Law enforcement officials protested that the ruling was unfair to them
as well. They feared that defendants whose trials occurred after *Miranda*
but who had been arrested before the landmark case would be freed
because police had not known at the time of arrest that they were supposed
to warn suspects of their rights.

In fact, most defendants were tried again and convicted. Miranda,
Vignera, and Westover quickly went to trial and were convicted.

At Miranda's second trial on February 24, 1967, the judge ruled no evidence could be used that was taken after his confession. But Miranda's girlfriend testified he had told her, during a visit in jail, that he had raped the victim. A jury of nine men and three women deliberated less than one hour before they found Miranda guilty. He received the same sentence as before—20 to 30 years in jail. During his appeal, Miranda had remained in jail, where he was serving time on an unrelated armed robbery charge.

Though critical of the *Miranda* ruling, Chief Assistant DA Burton B. Roberts of New York said only a few cases in his district had resulted in the freeing of criminals. He noted that the number of confessions by suspects in criminal cases "had not decreased appreciably."[2]

Studies of confessions after *Miranda* confirmed that assessment. A study conducted by Yale Law School students found that *Miranda* had little effect on police in New Haven, Connecticut. Despite the decision, suspects continued to confess after waiving their rights, according to the study. The students also found that most defendants pleaded guilty. Those cases that went to trial were almost always based on evidence even if confessions were used.[3]

These findings had far less impact on the public than the headlines reporting the few cases allowing suspects to go free. BRONX MAN WHO ADMITTED RAPE SET FREE UNDER MIRANDA RULING greeted readers of the February 28, 1967, edition of the *New York Times*.[4] The case involved Michael Stern, a twenty-one-year-old Bronx student, who had confessed raping a seventy-five-year-old woman in 1965. He was freed because he had not been advised of his rights and because his trial was held after *Miranda* was announced.

It was headlines like these that enraged the public. Politicians were quick to make use of anti-*Miranda* sentiment. In 1968, Congress passed the

Senator Sam Ervin Jr. led the attack against Justice Fortas.

Omnibus Crime Control and Safe Streets Act, which tried to overrule *Miranda*. The act said confessions could be used in federal court—as long as they were voluntary—even if police had failed to warn suspects of their rights. President Lyndon Johnson signed the bill but ordered the Justice Department to use only confessions allowed under *Miranda*.

Justice Fortas became an easy target for the anger directed at the Supreme Court when President Johnson nominated him to replace Earl Warren as Chief Justice in 1968. The justice had accepted $15,000 to teach a course at American University that summer, which many considered improper. Citing *Miranda*, Senator Sam Ervin Jr. led the attack against

Fortas in the Senate. As criticism mounted, Fortas asked that his nomination be withdrawn.

Richard M. Nixon, running for president in 1968, seized upon the public's resentment over the Warren Court rulings on suspects' rights. Basing his campaign on a "law-and-order" platform, he portrayed the Court and his opponent as soft on crime. Nixon told voters that he wanted to reverse *Miranda* and that he would appoint Supreme Court justices who would do it.

In March 1969, the Court ruled that police had to warn people of their rights as soon as they were in police custody, not just before questioning. White, who with Stewart issued a "heated dissent," said the new ruling "draws the straitjacket even tighter" on police efforts to fight crime.[5] Thurgood Marshall, who as solicitor general had argued against *Miranda*, voted with the majority. It was one of the last decisions of Chief Justice Warren, who retired from the Court in June 1969.

Fortas did not participate in the opinion. He was once again embroiled in a controversy, this time over his acceptance of a $20,000 honorarium, which he had arranged in 1965 but had returned 11 months later. In May 1969 Fortas resigned from the Court, the only justice in history to be forced to do so. Many blamed his troubles in part on *Miranda* and the public outrage it inspired toward the Court.

Once elected, Nixon tried to make good on his pledge to reverse *Miranda*. In May 1969, he nominated Warren E. Burger to fill the Chief Justice position. Burger, an outspoken critic of *Miranda*, had been known as a law-and-order judge when he served on the U.S. Circuit Court of Appeals for the District of Columbia. Nixon was to appoint three more conservative justices—Harry A. Blackmun, Lewis F. Powell Jr., and William H. Rehnquist—before resigning from office in 1974.

Richard Nixon used the public's outrage over the release of criminals after the *Miranda* ruling to win votes in his successful bid for the presidency in 1968.

Nixon attacked *Miranda* on another front as well. Speaking at a hearing of the Special House Commission on Crime in August 1969, Nixon's attorney general, John M. Mitchell, announced the Justice Department would no longer abide by *Miranda*. "If a federal official inadvertently fails to give a full warning," he told Congress, "the Department of Justice now believes the confession may still be a voluntary confession and should be presented to the court as evidence."[6] Nixon hoped to take a contested confessions case to the Supreme Court, where the new law-and-order majority would rule on it.

James Vorenberg, a Harvard law professor and director of President Lyndon Johnson's Crime Commission, called Mitchell's announcement a "dangerous hoax." He argued that the *Miranda* ruling was not to blame for the rising crime rate. *Miranda*, he said, affected only a fraction of 1 percent of the crimes reported. "It is a dangerous hoax for the Attorney General to suggest that if you fiddle with the Bill of Rights, you can cut down crime."[7]

The case of *Harris v. New York* gave the Burger Court its first chance to rule on *Miranda*. Viven Harris had been arrested in 1966 on a narcotics charge by police in New Rochelle, New York, before the *Miranda* ruling. Police did not warn him of his rights, and he confessed to the crime. During his trial, the court did not allow the confession to be used to prove Harris's guilt. But when Harris testified that he had not committed the crime, police used the confession to contradict his statements. The jury found him guilty, and Harris appealed. He claimed that, under the *Miranda* ruling, the illegally obtained confession should not have been used.

In a 5 to 4 ruling, issued February 24, 1971, the Court ruled that the police could use the confession to contradict the defendant's statements. Burger, who wrote the opinion, said *Miranda* "cannot be perverted into a license to use perjury."[8] It was more important to expose lies during the

Attorney General John M. Mitchell told Congress the Justice Department would not follow the *Miranda* ruling.

trial than to worry about the possibility that the ruling might encourage police to obtain statements illegally, Burger said.

The ruling infuriated Brennan, who with Douglas, Black, and Marshall dissented. "The Court today," he said in his dissent, "tells the police that they may freely interrogate an accused incommunicado and without counsel and know that . . . it may be introduced if the defendant has the temerity to testify in his own defense."[9]

The ruling weakened *Miranda*, but it did not overturn it. Harlan had convinced the Court to limit the ruling. Though a critic of *Miranda*, Harlan believed it was important not to ignore what past courts had decided. The

Court relied on precedence—cases already decided—in almost all its rulings.

After the *Harris* ruling, the assistant attorney general said the Justice Department would no longer try to find a test case to overturn *Miranda*.

Another test of *Miranda* came during the 1976 term when Robert Anthony Williams asked the Court to overturn his murder conviction. Williams had kidnapped a ten-year-old girl, sexually molested her, and thrown her body in a culvert. Police refused to allow Williams's lawyer to ride with him to jail. During the ride, Williams directed police to the girl's body. A federal appeals court overturned Williams's conviction on the grounds that his *Miranda* rights had been violated.

Twenty-one states joined Iowa in asking the Supreme Court to overturn the ruling. They argued that *Miranda* was "too restrictive" and "should be abandoned in favor of a more flexible standard."[10] In arguing his case, Iowa's attorney general asked the Court, "What is really wrong with tricking a man into telling the truth? That is one of the goals of a good Perry Mason-type cross-examination."[11]

The Court ruled in favor of Williams in a 5 to 4 decision issued March 23, 1977. The ruling was based not on *Miranda*'s warnings but on the right to counsel. Burger issued an emotional dissent, calling the ruling "weird." Stewart, who had opposed *Miranda*, wrote the majority opinion ordering a new trial for Williams. He was joined by Brennan, Marshall, Stevens, and Nixon-appointee Powell.

Since then, the Court has ruled on both sides of the issue of suspects' rights. In a 1980 case, *Rhode Island v. Innis*, the Court defined interrogation. It ruled that a suspect's rights were not violated when he led police to the murder weapon after a police officer's offhand remark. But the Court stressed that police remarks made to get the suspect to confess would be

Chief Justice Warren E. Burger

considered interrogation. Before making such remarks, the Court said, police would have to warn suspects of their rights.

Burger voted with the majority. In a separate opinion on the case, he wrote: "I would neither overrule *Miranda*, disparage it, nor extend it at this late date."[12]

On March 26, 1991, the Court ruled against suspects' rights in another Arizona case, *Arizona v. Fulminante*. The Court's 5 to 4 ruling said a defendant's conviction does not automatically have to be overturned because a forced confession was used at trial. But, it said, the use of the forced confession had to be proved to be "a harmless error." The Court added that there had to be enough evidence to convict the defendant without the confession.

Justice White, once a bitter foe of *Miranda*, issued a blistering dissent. The ruling, White wrote, discarded "one of the fundamental tenets of our criminal justice system"—the right not to be forced to testify against oneself.[13]

The *Miranda* warning, which tells suspects of their right to remain silent and to consult an attorney, has become part of everyday police procedure. Most people—who hear it every time they view a TV police show—can recite it as well as the "Pledge of Allegiance." Suspects everywhere have no doubt heard the warning long before police officers read it to them.

Though some police officials still grumble over the Court's rulings on suspects' rights, others have come to accept them as necessary. "We're a free country," said Police Lieutenant Louis Arcangeli of Atlanta, commenting in an article on suspects' rights 25 years after the *Miranda* decision. "While we wouldn't have crime if we were under martial law, I think that it is a tradeoff. We are free."[14]

Ernesto Miranda in 1967

Miranda and the other rulings on suspects' rights forced police to become better at collecting evidence, and led to a trained, sophisticated police force, according to other officials. "When *Miranda* came down," said Sheriff William Heafey of Nevada County, California, "all of law enforcement thought the bad guys had won again. But after some reluctance and suspicion, we just began to work harder. We became more professional. Instead of relying on outwitting somebody in an interrogation, we went and got good evidence."[15]

Miranda, the man whose name will be forever linked to suspects' rights, benefited little from the decision. Serving time at Arizona State Prison for rape, kidnapping, and robbery, he was referred to as "the" Miranda by both prisoners and guards.

In September 1971, Miranda, while still in prison, was convicted of the $8 robbery of a Phoenix bank worker in 1962. During the trial he was called "José Gomez," because the judge feared the jurors' minds "would be clouded" if they knew his true identity. After the trial, one juror remarked, "I think all of us kept wondering why the man was being tried for an $8 robbery that occurred in 1962."[16]

He was freed on parole on December 12, 1972. In a 1973 interview, he said he had completed two years of college while in prison and had a good job. He wouldn't say what the job was.

On July 13, 1974, police stopped Miranda's car for a traffic violation in Tempe, Arizona. Under the front seat, Patrolman Michael Breedlove found a gun and pills classified as a dangerous drug. Charges against Miranda were later dropped because police had failed to get a proper search warrant before searching his car. By the time the last charge was dismissed, on August 20, 1975, Miranda had served three and a half months in Arizona State Prison.

On January 31, 1976, a man stabbed Miranda in the chest and abdomen in a skid row bar in Phoenix, Arizona. A waitress there said Miranda and two men had had a fistfight over a card game. When Miranda returned from the bathroom after washing blood off his hands, one of the men attacked him. He died on the way to a Phoenix hospital. In Miranda's pocket, police found two cards with the *Miranda* warning printed on them. He had been selling them for $2 apiece near the county courthouse.

Police at the murder scene arrested Fernando Rodriguez Zamora, a twenty-three-year-old Mexican immigrant who witnesses said handed a knife to Miranda's killer. The arresting officer took one of Miranda's cards and read the warning to Zamora.

Source **N**otes

Introduction

1. *Mapp v. Ohio*, 367 US 643, p. 659.
2. *New York Times* (Feb. 1, 1976), p. 28.
3. Melvin M. Belli, *The Law Revolution (Volume One—Criminal Law)* (Los Angeles: Sherbourne Press, 1968), p. 62.

Chapter One

1. *Olmstead v. United States*, 277 US 438, p. 485.
2. *New York Times* (April 26, 1964), p. 69.
3. Ibid., p. 1.
4. Ibid.
5. Ibid., p. 69.
6. Ibid., p. 1.
7. Ibid., p. 69.
8. Ibid. (Jan. 27, 1965), p. 16.
9. Ibid.
10. Ibid. (Jan. 28, 1965), p. 17.
11. Ibid.
12. Ibid. (April 11, 1973), p. 1.
13. Ibid. (Jan. 30, 1965), p. 26.
14. Ibid. (Jan. 28, 1965), p. 17.
15. Fred P. Graham, *The Self-Inflicted Wound* (New York: Macmillan, 1970), p. 79.
16. *New York Times* (Jan. 30, 1965), p. 1.
17. Jethro K. Lieberman, *Milestones! Two Hundred Years of American Law* (New York: Oxford University Press, 1976), p. 333.

Chapter Two

1. Leonard W. Levy, ed., *The Supreme Court Under Earl Warren* (New York: New York Times Co., 1972), p. 167

2. Lieberman, p. 166.

3. Ibid., p. 167.

4. Ibid., p. 169.

5. Ibid.

6. Ibid., p. 236.

7. Ibid., p. 238.

8. Graham, p. 43.

Chapter Three

1. Richard J. Medalie, *From Escobedo to Miranda: The Anatomy of a Supreme Court Decision* (Washington, D.C.: Lerner Law Book, 1966), p. 12.

2. Lieberman, p. 328.

3. Ibid.

4. Belli, p. 58.

5. Graham, p. 163.

6. Lieberman, p. 329.

7. Medalie, p. 7.

8. Ibid., p. 11.

9. Ibid., p. 17.

10. Ibid., p. 24.

Chapter Four

1. Medalie, p. 235.

2. *New York Times* (Feb. 1, 1976), p. 28.

3. Ibid.

4. Medalie, p. 32.

5. Graham, p. 154.

6. Medalie, p. ix.

Chapter Five

1. Medalie, p. 120.

2. Witt, Elder, *Congressional Quarterly's Guide to the U.S. Supreme Court*, second edition (Washington, D.C.: Congressional Quarterly, 1990), p. 870.

3. Medalie, p. 79.

4. Ibid., p. 82.

5. Ibid., p. 83.

6. Ibid.

7. Ibid., p. 84.

8. Ibid., p. 87.

9. Ibid., p. 89.

10. Ibid., p. 90.

11. Ibid., p. 91.

12. Ibid., p. 92.

13. Ibid., p. 93.

14. Ibid., p. 94.

15. Ibid., p. 96.

16. Ibid., p. 100.

17. Ibid., p. 99.

18. Ibid., p. 102.

19. Ibid.

20. Ibid., p. 103.

21. Ibid., p. 104.

22. Ibid.

23. Ibid., p. 105.

24. Ibid., p. 107.

25. Ibid., p. 115.

26. Ibid., pp. 119-120.

27. Ibid., p. 121.

28. Ibid., pp. 137-138.

Chapter Six

1. Medalie, p. 14.

2. Ibid., p. 196.

3. Ibid., p. 221.

4. Ibid., p. 220.

5. *New York Times* (June 14, 1966), p. 25.

6. Lieberman, p. 334.

7. *New York Times* (June 14, 1966), p. 1.

8. Ibid.

9. Ibid.

10. *Miranda v. Arizona*, 384 US 436, p. 517.

11. Medalie, p. 272.

12. Ibid., pp. 299-300.

13. *New York Times* (June 14, 1966), p. 25.

14. James F. Simon, *In His Own Image: The Supreme Court in Richard Nixon's America* (New York: David McKay, 1973), p. 49.

15. Ibid.

16. New York T*imes* (June 14, 1966), p. 25.

17. Ibid.

Chapter Seven

1. *Snyder v. Massachusetts*, 291 US 97, p. 122.
2. *New York Times* (Feb. 28, 1967), p. 40.
3. Levy, p. 101.
4. *New York Times* (Feb. 28, 1967), p. 40.
5. Ibid. (March 26, 1969), p. 1.
6. Ibid. (Aug. 1, 1969), p. 38.
7. Ibid.
8. Ibid. (Feb. 25, 1971), p.1.
9. Ibid.
10. Ibid. (Oct. 4, 1976), p. 15.
11. Ibid.
12. Ibid. (May 13, 1980), p. 17.
13. Ibid. (March 27, 1991), p. 1.
14. *Life* (Fall Special 1991), vol. 14, issue 13, p. 87.
15. Ibid., pp. 86-87.
16. *New York Times* (Sept. 24, 1971), p. 82.

Further **R**eading

Belli, Melvin M. *The Law Revolution (Volume One—Criminal Law)*. Los Angeles: Sherbourne, 1968.

Clark, Ramsey, ed. *Crime and Justice*. New York: New York Times Co., 1974.

Coy, Harold, (revised by Lorna Greenberg.) *The Supreme Court*. New York: Watts, 1981.

David, Andrew. *Famous Supreme Court Cases*. Minneapolis: Lerner, 1980.

Douglas, Jack D., ed. *Crime and Justice in American Society*. New York: Macmillan, 1971.

Douglas, William O. *The Court Years, 1939-1975: The Autobiography of William O. Douglas*. New York: Random House, 1980.

Force, Eden. *The American Heritage History of the Bill of Rights: The Sixth Amendment*. Englewood Cliffs, New Jersey: Silver Burdett, 1991.

Forte, David F. The S*upreme Court*. New York: Watts, 1979.

Fribourg, Marjorie G. *The Supreme Court in American History: Ten Great Decisions—The People, the Times and the Issues*. Philadelphia: Macrae Smith, 1965.

Goldberg, Arthur J. *Equal Justice: The Warren Era of the Supreme Court*. New York: Farrar, Straus & Giroux, 1971.

Goode Stephen. *The Controversial Court: Supreme Court Influences on American Life*. New York: Messner, 1982.

Graham, Fred P. *The Self-Inflicted Wound*. New York: Macmillan, 1970.

Greene, Carol. *The Supreme Court.* Chicago: Childrens Press, 1985.

Habenstreit, Barbara. *Changing America and the Supreme Court.* New York: Julian Messner, 1970.

Harrison, Maureen and Steve Gilbert, ed. *Landmark Decisions of the United States Supreme Court.* Beverly Hills: Excellent Books, 1991.

Heilbroner, David. *Rough Justice: Days and Nights of a Young D.A.* New York: Pantheon, 1990.

Lawson, Don. *Landmark Supreme Court Cases.* Hillside, New Jersey: Enslow, 1987.

Lieberman, Jethro K. *Milestones! Two Hundred Years of American Law.* New York: Oxford University Press, 1976.

Marquardt, Dorothy A. *A Guide to the Supreme Court.* Indianapolis: Bobbs-Merrill, 1977.

Peterson, Helen Stone. *The Supreme Court in America's Story.* Scarsdale, New York: Garrard Publishing Co., 1976.

Sevilla, Charles M. *Disorder in the Court: Great Fractured Moments in Courtroom History.* New York: W. W. Norton, 1992.

Stein, R. Conrad. *The Story of the Powers of the Supreme Court.* Chicago: Childrens Press, 1989.

Tresolini, Rocco. *Historic Decisions of the Supreme Court.* Philadelphia: J.B. Lippincott, 1963.

Woodward, Bob, and Scott Armstrong. *The Brethren: Inside the Supreme Court.* New York: Avon Books, 1981.

Index